VIOLENCE ON AMERICA'S STREETS

Gene Brown

THE MILLBROOK PRESS

Brookfield, Connecticut

Published by The Millbrook Press
2 Old New Milford Road
Brookfield, CT 06804
© 1992 Blackbirch Graphics, Inc.
First Edition

Created and produced in association with Blackbirch Graphics.
Series Editor: Bruce S. Glassman

Library of Congress Cataloging-in-Publication Data
Brown, Gene.
     Violence on America's streets / Gene Brown.
     Includes index and bibliography.
     Summary: Discusses street crime, gun control, police brutality, and other aspects of crime and violence in modern America.
     1. Crime—United States—Juvenile literature. 2. Violence—United States—Juvenile literature [1. Crime. 2. Violence.] I. Title. II. Series.
     ISBN 1-878841-95-5 (pbk)
     HV6789.B76   1992
     364.1'0973—dc20   91-28929
                                                                       CIP
123456789 - WO - 96 95 94 93 92   AC

Acknowledgments and photo credits
Cover: ©David Murray/Stock South; p. 4: ©J.M. Giboux/Gamma-Liaison; pp. 6, 23: ©Wayne Miles/Gamma-Liaison; p.8: ©The Bettmann Archive; pp. 10, 14, 32: AP/Wide World Photos; p. 11: North Wind Picture Archives; p. 12: Photofest; p. 16: ©Michael Hirsch/Gamma-Liaison; pp. 17, 20, 42, 47: Wide World Photos; pp. 18, 19: ©Deborah Copaken/Gamma-Liaison; p. 24: ©Douglas Pizac/Wide World Photos; p. 25: ©B. Riha/Gamma-Liaison; p. 28: ©Lenox McClendon/Wide World Photos; pp. 29, 31, 59: Gamma-Liaison; pp. 36, 48, 50, 51 (bottom): ©John Chiasson/Gamma-Liaison; p. 38: ©Cynthia Johnson/Gamma-Liaison; p. 40: ©Nick/Wide World Photos; p. 41: ©Diana Walker/Gamma-Liaison; p. 51 (top): ©Kavork Djansezian/Wide World Photos; p. 52: ©Ron Edwards/Wide World Photos; p. 54: ©Raphael Gaillard/Gamma-Liaison; p. 55: ©Eric Vandeville/Gamma-Liaison; p. 57: ©Yvonne Hemsey/Gamma-Liaison.

Maps and charts by David Bell.

Special thanks to Cindy Dopkin and Elvis Brathwaite.

Contents

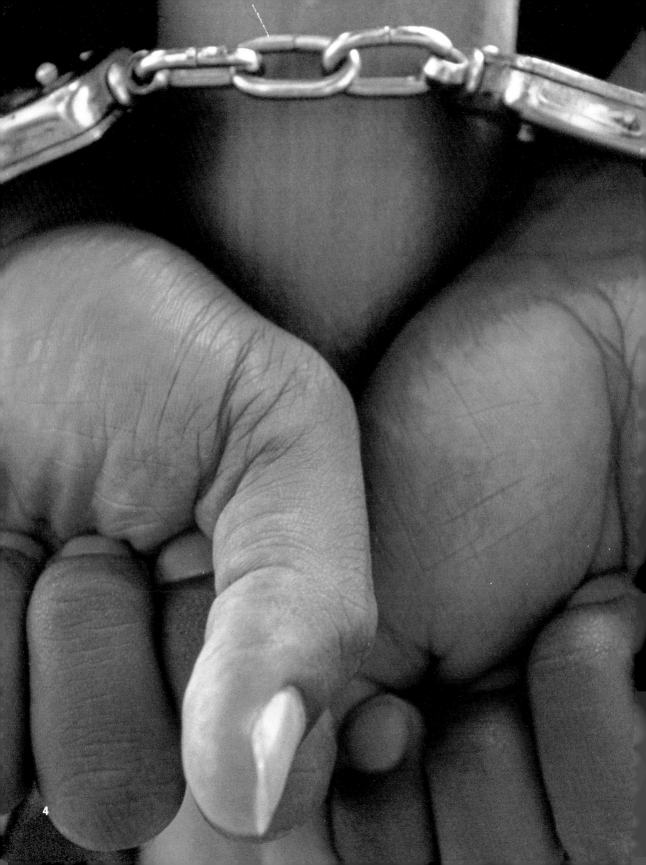

Chapter 1

The Violence Epidemic

No wonder people are afraid. In 1990, murderers took the lives of 23,438 Americans; there also were 102,555 rapes and 639,271 robberies reported in the United States.

It can happen to anyone, anywhere. In Los Angeles inner city areas, teachers hold "bullet drills." They teach children to drop to the ground if they hear shots. In Dallas, a major league baseball umpire was shot when he tried to stop a robbery.

Since the 1960s, violent crime has changed the way we live. Fear of crime has made us feel less free. People hesitate to go out at night, and more areas seem "off limits" because they are not safe. A 1989 poll asked people if there was anywhere within a mile of their home where they were afraid to walk. "Yes," said forty-three percent of those questioned. In a similar poll taken in 1967, only thirty-one percent gave that answer.

Many people carry knives or hidden guns for protection, even in states where it's illegal. Others carry a chemical that can disable an attacker when sprayed. And still others have learned karate for self-defense.

Crime is also expensive. Good locks are not cheap, nor are burglar alarm systems, which can cost thousands of dollars.

Fear of crime
has made us
feel less free

Opposite:
U.S. law enforcement officials make between 13 and 14 million arrests each year.

The cost of the government's fight on crime is ballooning out of control. We spend about $150 billion dollars a year on the police, courts, and prisons. That's about $200 per year for each person in the United States.

There is also an emotional price we pay for violent crime. A doctor who was mugged said that she "felt vulnerable, helpless, powerless, rage." Victims often become much more afraid than they used to be. They may not want to go out at all. Women who have been raped are sometimes left fearful of all men, even ones they know and care about. They often become depressed as well.

These crimes also divide Americans along racial lines. An unusually large number of people charged with violent crimes are minorities, as arrest figures and television and newspaper crime reports show. Blacks—and to a lesser extent Hispanics—seem to be involved in these crimes more often than their population suggests they would.

The victim of a Los Angeles gang war lies dead in front of a neighborhood liquor store.

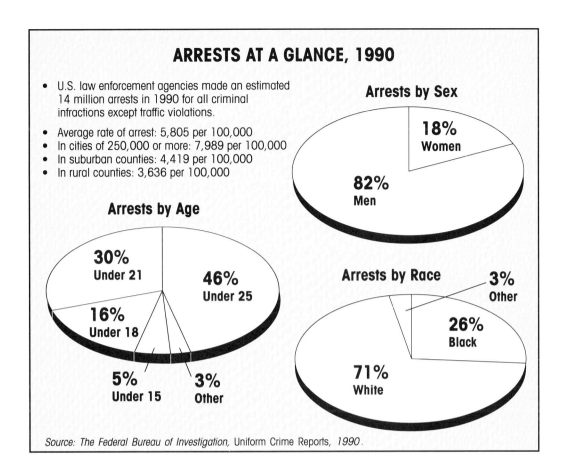

ARRESTS AT A GLANCE, 1990

- U.S. law enforcement agencies made an estimated 14 million arrests in 1990 for all criminal infractions except traffic violations.

- Average rate of arrest: 5,805 per 100,000
- In cities of 250,000 or more: 7,989 per 100,000
- In suburban counties: 4,419 per 100,000
- In rural counties: 3,636 per 100,000

Arrests by Sex

18% Women

82% Men

Arrests by Age

30% Under 21

46% Under 25

16% Under 18

5% Under 15

3% Other

Arrests by Race

3% Other

26% Black

71% White

Source: *The Federal Bureau of Investigation,* Uniform Crime Reports, *1990.*

There are many reasons for this, as we shall later see. Unfortunately, people often look at the news stories and think that there is only one reason. These people think somehow, "that's just the way *they* are." This attitude only worsens the problem of racism in America.

Questions in Need of Answers

Our parents and grandparents didn't grow up in such a violent world. What has changed since they were young?

What is the role of guns, drugs, poverty, and racism in this plague of violence?

There are more than a million people behind bars in the United States. No other country has as big a part of its population in jail or prison. Is this part of the solution? If not, then what?

Will anything stop the violence?

Chapter 2

How We Got There

Between 1960 and 1981, reports of serious offenses in the United States increased more than two hundred percent. By the early 1980s, many people could not remember a time when they felt safe to walk in the street at night. Then, in the mid-1980s, crack ignited a new round of violence that has not yet let up.

When did we get started on this trail of bloodshed, fear, and death? Were we always such a violent country?

We Americans have always felt that our society was freer and more open than others. From the beginning of our country, there were fewer customs, rules, and laws to control people's lives. People depended more on themselves, less on others. With vast amounts of land, they moved around a lot. The country grew and changed more than most other large nations. The frontier seemed never far away.

But this also made us a society with rough edges. With guns and knives plentiful, frontier justice was quick and often violent. Using these weapons was an easy way to settle an argument.

The big cities that grew rapidly in the nineteenth century also seemed like frontiers. In 1868, for example, *The New York Times* wrote: "There is hardly a day in which the pistol or the knife is not used against human life."

Violence has been part of American society for generations

Opposite:
Law enforcement in the nineteenth century was often characterized by a single policeman walking a beat. Here, a typical city officer speaks with a shoeshine boy in 1897.

By 1900, poor immigrants who lived in the cities in large numbers were being blamed for crime. Sometimes the Italians were blamed. The Jews and the Irish were also singled out. In fact, poor Irish-Americans were once called "the dangerous class."

In the 1920s, America was hit by a crime wave. The sale of alcoholic drinks had been banned by the Eighteenth Amendment to the Constitution, which was also known as Prohibition. But many people still wanted to drink. Although illegal, liquor was still available. Gangsters controlled it and fought over who would sell it and where. It was much like the warfare between today's drug gangs. Perhaps the most famous of the Prohibition gangsters was Chicago's Al Capone.

In the 1930s, bank robbers caused another crime wave. Outlaws such as John Dillinger and Bonnie and Clyde captured the headlines. They had running battles with FBI agents, who were known as "G-men."

Chicago's Al Capone, kingpin of the illegal liquor trade during the 1920s, was one of America's most famous criminals.

Frontier Violence

The great open spaces and long distances between towns made it easy for outlaws to rob, murder, and hide on the frontier. Billy the Kid, for instance, murdered twenty-one people before being cut down himself at age twenty-two by a sheriff's bullet.

Law enforcement wasn't mild-mannered either. For example, Judge Roy Bean relied as much on his pistol as on his one law book to hand down justice in the Texas town of Langtrey. When a law enforcement official could not be found, citizens often took the law into their own hands. Vigilantes frequently dispensed justice with a noose.

The South and the West were on the leading edge of the ever-expanding frontier. Today, we still feel this heritage. America's South still has the highest murder rate in the nation. The Western states have the highest rate of all violent crimes.

Arguments in the Old West were commonly settled with guns.

While newspapers used words like "epidemic" to describe crime in these years, the crime rate was mild by today's standards. We don't have accurate crime statistics for this period, but the FBI's best figures show that the rate of violent crime is possibly more than a hundred times worse today than it was in the 1930s.

During World War II, in the 1940s, newspapers reported outbreaks of teenage crime. One reason given for this flare-up was that parents were often not around to supervise their children. Many fathers were in the military, and mothers worked in war plants.

As it does today, Los Angeles had a problem with youth gangs that often dressed in a special way. They wore "zoot suits" with baggy pants. Sometimes they used guns.

This pattern of youth crime did not go away. By the 1950s people were worried about juvenile delinquency. Gangs of teenagers in many cities fought each other to control neighborhoods. Nothing seemed to work to stop this street warfare.

Americans became increasingly aware of youth crime and juvenile delinquency in the 1950s. The movie classic *West Side Story* was one of the first films to depict these growing problems in our society.

Crime in Our Time

The picture of crime in the streets as we know it began to take shape in the 1960s. Increasingly, drugs—their sale and use—were involved. As in Prohibition in the 1920s, gangs began to fight over who would be able to sell drugs in a particular area. Addicts needed large amounts of money to buy drugs and many got it by robbing. Heroin was the drug they often used.

Until then, violent crime seemed to happen mostly in poorer neighborhoods when the violence was directed by one gang at another. In general, "civilians" felt safe and violent crime never seemed to get totally out of control.

But by the 1960s, the fear of violence was spreading. It seemed that there was no longer such a thing as a "safe neighborhood" in big cities. And it was even beginning to touch the suburbs. Not only was crime spreading, it was becoming more violent.

Television and magazines like *Time* and *Newsweek* gave more coverage to the problem. People began to talk more about it. For the first time violent crime also became a major political issue. The 1964 Republican presidential candidate, Barry Goldwater, a conservative, made the growing crime rate a central issue in his campaign and assailed the Democrats for not being tough enough on the issue.

In the mid-1960s, riots occurred in many inner city neighborhoods. The civil rights movement was finally bringing freedoms to blacks that other Americans always took for granted. But, if anything, this made many people in the ghettos feel even more frustrated than before. They felt that the police still treated them in a racist manner. And while the rest of America prospered, millions of black people seemed stuck forever in the slums.

Many white people couldn't understand why riots were happening in black neighborhoods. It made them angry. They tied the rioting to the rising tide of muggings, which they also associated with blacks. Fear for their safety made many whites lose interest in *why* this was happening; they just wanted it to end.

Everyone seemed to know someone whose purse had been snatched, or who had been hurt in a mugging. Something seemed to have gone terribly wrong with America. There was a widespread demand that the streets be made safer and that those who broke the law be severely punished. The public wanted "law and order."

Richard Nixon was one of the first politicians to make the fight against "crime in the streets" a national campaign issue.

The National Commission on the Causes and Prevention of Violence, set up by President Johnson, reported that American cities were becoming "places of terror." In a speech to Congress, the president denounced "rising crime and lawlessness" in the country.

In 1968, Republican presidential candidate Richard Nixon said he spoke for "the silent majority" who wanted an end to "crime in the streets." His running mate, Spiro Agnew, kept pressing the issue. He attacked the criminal justice system which, he said, favored the criminals over the victims.

The Supreme Court came under fire. It had recently handed down decisions aimed at protecting the rights of those suspected of crimes. Many people felt that this was "handcuffing" the police, making it harder for them to protect the public.

The states passed tougher criminal laws, and many cities elected conservative mayors. For example, in 1971, Philadelphia elected as mayor its police commissioner, Frank

Rizzo. Describing himself as "the toughest cop in America," Rizzo declared: "The streets are safe in Philadelphia, it's only the people who make them unsafe."

But as the 1970s wore on, street crime worsened. In one dramatic example, in 1973, Senator John Stennis of Mississippi was shot in the chest in front of his Washington, D.C., home in an attempted robbery.

The 1980s

By the beginning of the 1980s, many people felt that neither the police nor the courts could protect them. Some were willing to take matters into their own hands.

An incident on a New York City subway in 1984 caused a national debate on the issue. And it again raised the question of race. On that day in 1984, four young black men approached a white man named Bernhard Goetz and asked him for money. Goetz, thinking that they were threatening him, pulled out a pistol and fired at them, leaving one man permanently paralyzed. Goetz did not have a license for the gun.

When the police set up a phone number to receive any information the public could supply about the crime, they were surprised at the response. Many callers simply wanted to express support for the gunman. The Guardian Angels, a private group of young people who rode the subways to stop crime before it happened, also backed Goetz.

Popular *Chicago Tribune* columnist Mike Royko had himself recently been robbed. He wrote about the Goetz incident: "The four punks looked for trouble and they found it. Case closed." Soon after, a *New York Times* poll showed that even a majority of black people supported what Goetz had done.

Those who opposed Goetz pointed out that if people started to take the law into their own hands, there would be chaos. Besides, how could Goetz be so sure that the four were going to hurt him? He had set himself up as the jury, judge, and executioner. He was promoting lawlessness as much as any criminal.

Although the rate of violent crime seemed to dip a bit as America moved further into the 1980s, it soon increased again. Drugs appeared to have a lot to do with the growth. A new drug appeared to be behind the surge in violence: crack, a smokable form of cocaine.

In the 1988 presidential election, George Bush made the threat of crime a major issue. His opponent, Michael Dukakis, was governor of Massachusetts. Bush's campaign ads, claiming that Dukakis was soft on crime, blamed him for allowing a man named Willie Horton to commit several violent crimes.

Horton was serving a life term for robbery and murder. Massachusetts law said that prisoners who had a record of good behavior could get furloughs, or temporary releases,

In 1984, Bernhard Goetz made national headlines by shooting at four youths who were trying to mug him on a New York subway.

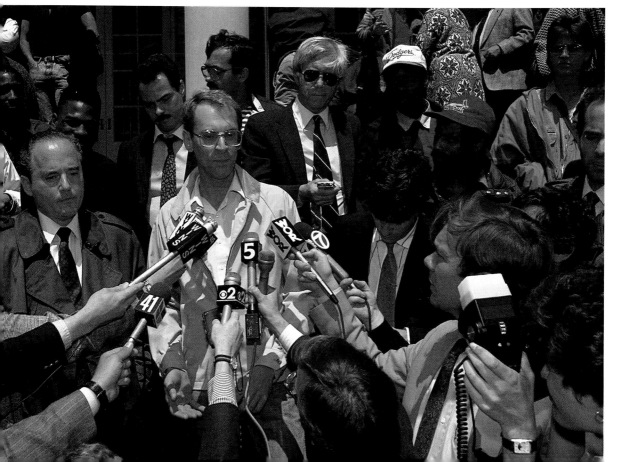

The Guardian Angels

Is it ever right for people to take the law into their own hands? In many neighborhoods, residents have set up patrols to watch for crime. Sometimes they carry radios to keep in touch with each other. If they see a crime taking place, they call the police. If necessary, they can stop someone who is breaking the law and hold him or her for the police. This is called a citizen's arrest.

In New York City in 1979, one group made this a city-wide, ongoing activity. They called themselves the Guardian Angels. The Angels were mostly black and Hispanic youths who felt that the police weren't able to protect the public. Wearing red berets and white t-shirts, about one-thousand of them patrolled high-crime areas and the subways, watching for trouble. They were unarmed, but skilled in the martial arts.

Curtis Sliwa, then twenty-four years old, founded the Guardian Angels. At first the police were hostile to his group. In fact, they arrested some Guardian Angels, claiming they had started fights. But eventually the police established an uneasy truce with them.

Curtis Sliwa and his wife, Lisa, also a Guardian Angel, then started similar groups in many other cities.

Sometimes, as in Miami and New Orleans, city officials welcomed them. Elsewhere, as in Chicago, they were opposed. There, the police chief called them a "goon squad." To that, Curtis Sliwa quickly responded: "If we weren't around, no one would be."

Lisa Sliwa (foreground) and her husband Curtis head the Guardian Angels.

lasting forty-eight hours. Horton, while on a furlough in 1986, raped a woman and stabbed a man.

Dukakis pointed out that more than forty states had similar laws. He also reminded Bush that California had used this program when Ronald Reagan was governor of that state.

Many people thought that the Willie Horton issue was really about race. Horton is black. They said that Republicans were trying to appeal to white fears. Lee Atwater was the man who ran the Bush campaign. A few years later, Atwater learned he was dying from a brain tumor. He said then that perhaps he had overdone the Horton issue. He apologized for any racism tied to it.

In 1989, a brutal crime shocked Americans. A woman who was jogging was raped and almost beaten to death in a park in New York City by a band of youths. They said they were "wilding"—out in a group, running wild, doing whatever they wanted to do. They attacked at random, overwhelming their victims. Often, they tortured, beat, robbed, and raped their victims. All in the name of fun.

Why Do People Join Gangs?

For some young people, joining a gang is an act of self-defense. With so many others in their neighborhood in gangs, young people feel they need protection. Unfortunately, as they quickly discover, membership produces a different kind of danger. Being in a gang makes a boy or girl the "enemy" to people in other gangs.

Money is another reason for joining. The unemployment rate for ghetto teenagers sometimes reaches twenty-five percent. But there's always work in the drug trade—and it always pays very well. Where else can an eighteen-year-old earn enough to drive a Mercedes?

Gangs also provide a "family." They arise in neighborhoods where there are many children from broken homes. The gang provides a feeling of belonging. Gang members are supposed to take care of each other, like family.

Gang members wear the same colors. The Crips, for example, wear blue so members can easily spot each other on the street. The colors are also like a badge of belonging, making each member feel important. It's a feeling they think they can't get any other way.

Almost anything can touch off violence between gangs, even the showing of films about gangs. In 1991, *New Jack City*, a movie about gangs and crack, sparked violence in several cities, including a fatal shooting.

A few months later it happened again when *Boyz N The Hood,* a specifically anti-gang film, opened. This movie ended with the words "Increase the Peace" spelled out on the screen. Two people died in fighting in several cities, causing some theaters to stop showing the film. Some people said that *Boyz N The Hood* caused the violence. Its twenty-three-year-old director, John Singleton, replied: "I didn't create the conditions under which people shoot each other." Others suggested that the violence was caused when one gang came to theaters on another gang's "turf."

Although the majority of organized gangs are all male, many female gangs exist in the United States.

The 1980s saw a great rise in violent crime due to gangs. Today, America's largest and most powerful gangs are responsible for much of the country's drug trafficking activity.

The fate of the "Central Park Jogger" touched Americans everywhere. It also reminded them that it could happen to anyone, any time, anywhere. And again, the issue of race came up. The attackers were black. The victim was white.

In many cities, gangs continued to be a problem. By the late 1980s, several hundred young people in Los Angeles were being killed each year in gang warfare. Some gangs in South Central Los Angeles, such as the Crips and the Bloods, have many thousands of members each. They are armed and deal in drugs.

In 1990, violent crime in America increased eleven percent. The nation seemed to be stuck with its problem. This left many Americans angry and baffled. They wanted to know why it was happening. And they wanted something done about it.

Chapter 3

The Causes

n 1988, when seven people in Great Britain were killed by handguns, 8,915 were shot to death in the United States. On the average, about 9,200 Americans are murdered with handguns each year. To much of the world, America still seems gripped by the violent spirit of the Wild West.

"Why are Americans so criminal?" the British magazine *The Economist* asked in 1990. It is one of the most respected publications in the world. The magazine pointed out that the murder rate in the United States is four to five times higher than it is in Western Europe. Rape is seven times higher, mugging as much as ten times higher.

Guns

Experts have given several reasons for our high rate of violent crime. *The Economist* focused on one. Americans are not necessarily more violent than other nationalities," it said, "it's just that they are armed."

Guns are much harder to get in Britain than they are in the United States. In Britain, they are strictly regulated.

The choice of a weapon makes a big difference. It is easier to hurt or kill someone with a pistol than with a knife or club. Criminals can kill with a gun without getting near enough to their victim to get hurt themselves.

Many say that guns, drugs, and poverty are the most potent factors in America's violence profile

Opposite:
More than $500,000 in cash is displayed at the offices of a Florida drug enforcement coalition. The cash, along with two tons of cocaine, was seized from a suburban home in Florida's wealthy Broward County.

This is true unless the intended victim also is armed.

Handguns are used in more than 600,000 crimes each year in our country. There are an estimated thirty to fifty million of these weapons in the United States. The number increases by about two million every year.

Americans have always felt strongly about having the right to own guns. Perhaps it is because of our frontier history. Firearms have been regulated, but mostly on the local level. So even when some cities have made it hard to buy a gun, a person could always get it from somewhere else in the country:

Drugs

Many law enforcement officials blame crack and other drugs for much of the violent crime that plagues America. Worries about drugs used to focus on addiction and the destruction of family life. The tie between drugs and violent crime is more recent. In the 1940s and 1950s, gangs—including the Mafia—fought over the control of the sale of narcotics. But they usually did not bother the public.

Increased use of heroin, especially in the 1960s, changed this. Heroin is expensive and very addictive. People on it need to keep using it; otherwise, they crash. Few people earn enough to pay for it, so many people steal to get the money to buy the drug.

At first, addicts, who usually lived in poor neighborhoods, stole from their neighbors. But eventually they began to break into houses and apartments everywhere. They also robbed from people on the streets. Much of the mugging that made headlines in the 1960s was caused by addicts needing money for drugs. In 1973, President Nixon called drugs "public enemy number one."

By the mid-1980s, another drug pushed into the spotlight. First it was cocaine in the form of white powder. Users sniffed it. Then the problem got worse.

Opposite:
Semiautomatic weapons and handguns are used in hundreds of thousands of crimes each year in America. Drug-dealing gangs often rely on the deadly efficiency of high-tech weapons to maintain control of their turf.

By the second half of the 1980s, crack, a more dangerous form of cocaine, appeared. Crack is cheaper and it can be smoked. Unlike heroin, crack makes people violent. It is said to produce edgy, tense, "wired" behavior. People on crack may be spoiling for a fight.

Shootings became common between rival crack dealers. Like the gangsters during Prohibition, the dealers fought over who would get to sell the drug and where. But now more than then, innocent people got caught in the crossfire.

The police in Washington, D.C., say that drugs are responsible for eighty percent of the murders in that city. Between 1985, when crack was introduced there, and 1989, the murder rate in Washington, D.C., jumped 151 percent.

Los Angeles police officials relate the details of a drug bust that yielded nearly one thousand pounds of cocaine. The seizure was one of the largest in recent California history.

About two-thirds of all inmates in state prisons used drugs in the weeks before they committed their latest crimes. Drug use among prisoners convicted of violent crimes was even slightly higher.

But while these figures show that drugs are strongly connected to crime, they don't prove that drugs *cause* crime. People on drugs commit crimes; people also commit crimes to get drugs. Exactly what is the role of drugs in criminal activity? Cause and effect has not been proved. One study even shows that the use of major drugs such as heroin or cocaine seems to start only after a person has already committed a few crimes.

The age profile of America's criminals gets lower as each decade passes. Today, young men between the ages of fifteen and twenty-four commit the majority of crimes in the United States.

Values

Is the outbreak of violent crime caused by a breakdown of American values? Conservatives say, "What happened to the difference between right and wrong?" Many parents, it seems, no longer teach it to their children.

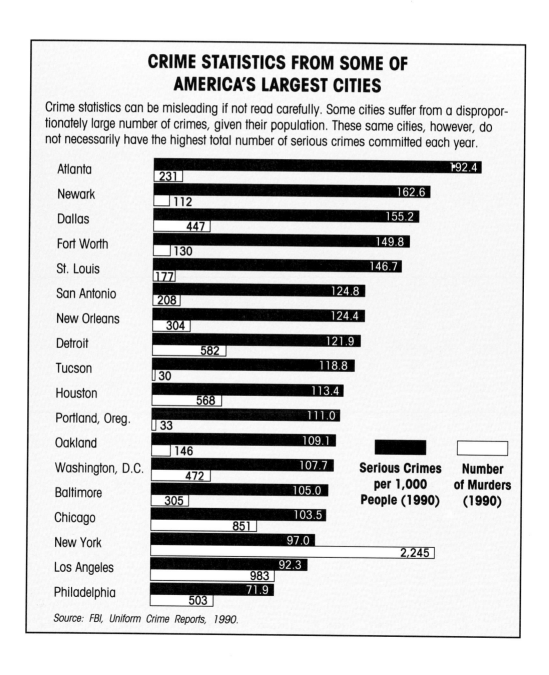

CRIME STATISTICS FROM SOME OF AMERICA'S LARGEST CITIES

Crime statistics can be misleading if not read carefully. Some cities suffer from a disproportionately large number of crimes, given their population. These same cities, however, do not necessarily have the highest total number of serious crimes committed each year.

City	Serious Crimes per 1,000 People (1990)	Number of Murders (1990)
Atlanta	192.4	231
Newark	162.6	112
Dallas	155.2	447
Fort Worth	149.8	130
St. Louis	146.7	177
San Antonio	124.8	208
New Orleans	124.4	304
Detroit	121.9	582
Tucson	118.8	30
Houston	113.4	568
Portland, Oreg.	111.0	33
Oakland	109.1	146
Washington, D.C.	107.7	472
Baltimore	105.0	305
Chicago	103.5	851
New York	97.0	2,245
Los Angeles	92.3	983
Philadelphia	71.9	503

Source: FBI, Uniform Crime Reports, 1990.

Changes in the family may be a factor. Higher rates of divorce and single parenthood leave children less supervised. They don't have as much guidance as they did in the past. They grow up with less discipline.

Respect for and concern with others seem to have decreased. People in our society are often isolated from each other, withdrawing into their own lives. Longstanding social ties are weaker here than in other societies. People move so much that it's hard to develop a feeling of community. They may not know or care much about their neighbors. According to sociologist Philip Slater, "We seek more and more privacy, and feel more and more alienated and lonely when we get it."

We don't seem to want to take responsibility for each other or to "get involved." This makes it easier for crime to grow. When someone is threatened by a criminal, strangers nearby may not want to help. They are afraid for their own safety so they turn away.

Is It a Matter of Age?

Some experts say that the cause of the wave of violent crime has to do with the age of people who commit crimes. They point out that young men ages fifteen to twenty-four commit most of the serious crimes in America. (Men are arrested ten times more often than women for violent crimes.)

This age group has made up an usually large part of the American people for the past two decades. The reason for this was the "baby boom," the large number of births that occurred between 1946 and 1964.

The first baby boomers reached age fifteen in 1961. The last turned twenty-four in 1988. If this theory is right, violent crime should have peaked between 1961 and 1988, when there were many people between the ages of fifteen and twenty-four. That did happen, but in the 1990s we haven't grown out of the problem. There are still plenty of young men committing crimes.

Could the increased violence since the mid-1980s be temporary? Did it happen only because of the crack epidemic? Had it not been for crack, would the age theory have proven itself? It's too soon to know. If we get crack under control and there is less violent crime in the future, the age of the population may have been at least part of the reason for our problem.

Race and Poverty

The number of children growing up in poverty in America increased by fifty percent between 1969 and 1990. Many say that this is at the heart of the rise in violent crime. As

Teen hotlines that offer help and advice to teens in distress have helped to keep many young people out of serious trouble.

Opposite:
Poverty-stricken neighborhoods in America's largest cities have traditionally been the battlegrounds for most violent crime.

California Congressman George Miller put it: "for the poor, violence has become a survival skill."

The rate of poverty is highest for certain ethnic and racial minorities. And they have the highest rates of violent crime on a per capita basis.

The FBI no longer classifies arrests by ethnic origins. In 1986, the last year it did, Hispanics accounted for 14.7 percent of all arrests for violent crimes. But they make up only eight percent of the population.

Even more dramatic are the statistics for black Americans. They make up twelve percent of the population. But almost fifty percent of those serving time in state prisons for violent crimes are black.

(We have to be careful with these numbers. Professor Evan Stark of Rutgers University says that police are more likely to charge black teenagers with a felony than they are white teenagers. Stark also says that courts are more likely to convict and imprison black teenagers than they are whites.)

Blacks in America

What is the reason for the extra-high black crime rate? It is to be found in a history that is different from that of any other group of people who came to this country.

Unlike other minorities, blacks were not only poor when they came here, they were enslaved. They had no control over any part of their lives. Their owners could and did split up and sell families. There were even laws in the South that made it a crime to teach a slave to read.

The Civil War freed the slaves, but blacks remained at the bottom of society. They owned almost no property. Prejudice against their skin color kept them from getting good jobs when they qualified. Separate and poor school systems—especially in the South, where most blacks lived—kept many blacks from making progress.

The children of white immigrants got better educations and better jobs than their parents. They moved out of the

Miami police officers check in with some local youths while on patrol in one of the city's troubled neighborhoods.

slums to better neighborhoods, joining the middle class. Many fewer blacks could look forward to their children doing this.

After World Wars I and II, many blacks moved to northern cities to take new factory jobs that had opened up—even to them. But prejudice and poverty kept most of them living in slums.

By the 1960s, blacks were pushing hard for equal rights. They took a new pride in their race. Black people would no longer take second place. Anger and rage at terrible treatment over the years surfaced. Now, when they felt that the police mistreated them, some rioted. With frustration growing and their futures bleak, the number of violent crimes committed by blacks began to rise.

In the mid-1960s laws were passed making many kinds of discrimination illegal. Special programs aimed to help blacks get a better education and jobs with a future. The idea was to make up for the kind of prejudice that blacks had suffered.

Over the next twenty years many blacks rose into the middle class. But many others were left behind in the slums. For them, there seemed to be no future. The kinds of jobs that once provided at least a survival income disappeared. The new jobs required skills—with computers, for example—that many poor blacks lacked.

Middle-class blacks might have helped to steady ghetto areas. But they moved out as soon as they could. For the poor and unskilled left behind, social problems seemed to feed on each other. Poverty made it hard to keep families together. Despair brought greater use of drugs. Young people were having children when they themselves were barely out of childhood. Welfare was often the only source of income.

Social scientists said that these people had become an "underclass." They could not even begin to climb the ladder to a better life. They seemed stuck where they were.

These are some of the sociological explanations for the high black crime rate in America. Though they only provide some of the answers, these explanations put the story of blacks and crime in a historical perspective.

By the end of the 1980s, blacks committing crimes against other blacks had become a deadly problem. The murder rate for black youths ages fifteen to nineteen doubled from 1984 to 1988. By 1990, one out of every one thousand black males ages fifteen to twenty-four was being murdered each year. That's ten times the rate for white males of the same age. There were more black men in prison cells than on college campuses.

A way had to be found to reduce the violence. Otherwise, a large part of a generation of young black men would either be killed or imprisoned.

Opposite:
State troopers in Alabama stood shoulder to shoulder on the steps of the Montgomery state capitol building in March of 1965. It was there that thousands of civil rights demonstrators—led by Dr. Martin Luther King, Jr.—ended their fifty-four-mile march to protest discrimination against blacks.

Selling Crack to America

Crack was neither invented nor "discovered." It was created by a shrewd crowd of drug-gang "marketeers" who took a simple production technique and made a low cost, ready-to-consume version of a powerful drug. Crack—which is smoked—delivered an instant and intense "high," adding to the drug's appeal. By the late 1980s, crack had become the most dangerous drug on America's streets. Its use and sale caused—directly and indirectly—a great rise in America's violent crime rate for that decade.

A Short History

Before crack, there was coca paste and cocaine freebase. Coca paste is an inexpensive, first-stage form of cocaine that comes in a powder. First reports of coca paste use came from Peru in 1971. By 1974, Lima, Peru, faced a coca-paste-smoking problem. By 1980, the epidemic had spread throughout neighboring Colombia, Bolivia, Ecuador, and Venezuela. From Colombia, refined coca paste began to make its way to Florida via the Caribbean.

During the early 1970s, American drug users began experimenting with freebasing cocaine—making a more pure and much more potent drug through various chemical processes. These early recipes for freebasing called for elaborate and very dangerous procedures.

By the late 1970s, demand on the streets was for a safer and simpler way to consume cocaine. In response to this consumer pressure, dealers intensified their search for new freebasing techniques and simpler packaging. What they finally came up with was crack. "They tried to figure out an efficient way to create large batches of cocaine freebase and then package it in such a way that it could be sold in a retail market," explained Bruce Johnson of Narcotic and Drug Research, Inc. of New York. Crack came in little "rocks" that could be packaged easily in small, easy-to-hide containers.

"Rock" Hits the West Coast

Crack arrived in Los Angeles around 1980. Two years later, Los Angeles hospital emergency rooms reported a ninety-percent increase in cocaine overdoses; the highest increase ever recorded. By 1983, "rock houses" first appeared.

Beginning in 1984, the rise of crack in American cities skyrocketed to incredible proportions. Sales of $25 cocaine "rocks" swept through Los Angeles accompanied by dozens of crack houses that seemed to appear

THE SPREAD OF CRACK IN AMERICA

Seattle
Portland
Minneapolis
Reno
Salt Lake City
Sacramento
Omaha
Rochester
Buffalo
York
Cleveland
Boston
Hartford
New York
Columbus
Philadelphia
Denver
Kansas City
Martinsburg
Baltimore
Las Vegas
St. Louis
Roanoke
Washington, D.C.
Los Angeles
Charlotte
Norfolk
San Diego
Oklahoma City
Atlanta
Wilmington, NC
Phoenix
Tucson
Dallas
Shreveport
Jamaican posses' overseas smuggling routes
Houston
MEXICO
Miami

JAMAICA

Outposts of Jamaican posses

Crips and Bloods controlled

overnight. At the same time, crack began to take firm hold in Miami and New York, and was often sold even more cheaply than on the West Coast. Supply almost could not keep up with the demand. As the crack business boomed, so did the dealers. They soon became "crack retailers," with brand names such as "Rambo" and "Miami Vice" that customers recognized and returned to.

One of crack's tightest strangleholds was the Washington Heights area in northern Manhattan. When night fell on this distinctly Caribbean neighborhood, many of the streets became choked with traffic. Some seventy to eighty percent of the customers jamming the avenues were white professionals from suburban New Jersey, Westchester, and Long Island. Washington Heights was an easy drive uptown for these customers, who then took their drugs to other destinations for consumption.

The Growth of Big Business

The crack market grew through 1985 and 1986. By the fall of 1986, the National Cocaine Hotline estimated that one million American had tried crack. As the crack business mushroomed, creating larger and larger profits, bigger crack organizations began to muscle out the small-time dealers. These organizations had corporate officers, distributors, lab operators, runners, enforcers, and street dealers who used high-tech equipment such as message beepers and mobile phones.

The Gangs Move In

As destructive and effective as the crack mega-organizations were in America's big cities, it took large, well-organized gangs to introduce crack to the rest of the country. These gangs—the major ones based on each coast—worked inland, competing with rivals for the largest share of the market. From the West Coast came the L.A.-based Crips (today about 30,000 strong) and the Bloods (about 9,000 members). In 1991, the Justice Department reported that Crips and Bloods were known to be in thirty-two states and 113 cities. Some experts think these two gangs control up to thirty percent of America's crack trade.

From the East Coast, Jamaican gangs—also known as "posses"—took control of spreading crack throughout the region. After locking in control of Miami, New York, and other major cities, the posses began concentrating on smaller cities and suburbs. More than forty different posses are known to exist today, with a total membership of more than 22,000. Officials at the Bureau of Alcohol, Tobacco, and Firearms (ATF) estimate that the Jamaican posses control another third of the country's crack trade. These gangs are known for their ruthless tactics and rampant use of violence. Since 1985, the ATF has documented over three-thousand posse-related homicides nationwide.

Officials estimate that there are approximately half a million crack-dependent people in America today. These statistics

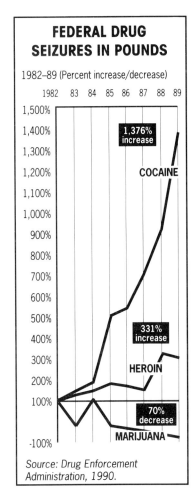

FEDERAL DRUG SEIZURES IN POUNDS

1982–89 (Percent increase/decrease)

1,376% increase

COCAINE

331% increase

HEROIN

70% decrease

MARIJUANA

Source: Drug Enforcement Administration, 1990.

are, of course, skewed on the low end since many serious drug users have "dropped out of sight" and can rarely be counted. Many others do not readily admit to a drug problem. The scourge of violent crime and drug dependency created by the spread of crack continues to destroy many of America's inner cities. Each year, thousands of innocent teenagers and young adults who live in those cities must struggle to avoid the catastrophic consequences of this powerful and dangerous epidemic.

Chapter 4

The Criminal Justice System

T he jails and prisons are jammed. In the 1980s, the federal prison population doubled. As the decade ended, state spending for prisons was increasing at a faster rate than for any other activity. These prisons were twenty-three percent over capacity. Half the state systems were under court order to reduce overcrowding.

Slightly more than five percent of all the people in the United States is arrested each year. In 1990, federal prisons held 65,526 inmates; 705,717 were locked up in state penitentiaries. California, alone, has 100,000 inmates—42,000 more people than the population of the state capital, Sacramento.

The criminal justice system, America's first line of defense against crime, put these people behind bars. It includes the police, the courts, and the prisons. But our defense appears to have broken down. Why hasn't it been able to stop violent crime?

The Police

When crime increases, the first thing people often say is "we need more police." But we can afford just so many of them. We also need to spend money on hospitals, schools, and roads.

Slightly more than five percent of all the people in the United States is arrested each year

Opposite:
The surge in America's prison population during the 1980s created an overcrowding problem of massive proportions.

Would more police do a better job if we were willing and able to pay the cost? Not necessarily. A police officer in Oakland, California, puts it bluntly: "Don't say give me more cars, give me more guns, give me more cops. That's been tried before, and it doesn't work."

How about putting the cop back on the beat? This is how the police mostly worked until the 1950s. In many places foot patrols are replacing cruising police cars.

This practice helps the officers and the people on their beat to get to know each other. People are more likely to

Many city police departments are returning to the old-fashioned system of "the cop on the beat." This kind of patrol enables officers to become familiar with the inner workings of a community and allows them to better anticipate problems before they arise.

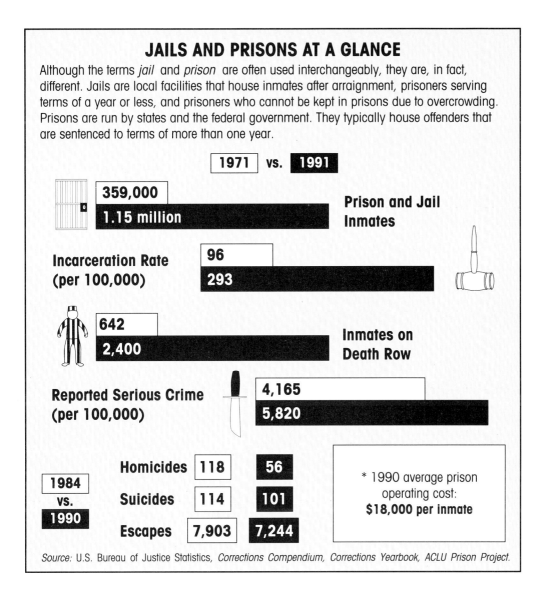

JAILS AND PRISONS AT A GLANCE

Although the terms *jail* and *prison* are often used interchangeably, they are, in fact, different. Jails are local facilities that house inmates after arraignment, prisoners serving terms of a year or less, and prisoners who cannot be kept in prisons due to overcrowding. Prisons are run by states and the federal government. They typically house offenders that are sentenced to terms of more than one year.

1971 vs. **1991**

	1971	1991
Prison and Jail Inmates	359,000	1.15 million
Incarceration Rate (per 100,000)	96	293
Inmates on Death Row	642	2,400
Reported Serious Crime (per 100,000)	4,165	5,820

1984 vs. **1990**

	1984	1990
Homicides	118	56
Suicides	114	101
Escapes	7,903	7,244

* 1990 average prison operating cost: **$18,000 per inmate**

Source: U.S. Bureau of Justice Statistics, *Corrections Compendium, Corrections Yearbook, ACLU Prison Project.*

cooperate with the police when they know them personally. The police also get to know the people better. In rough neighborhoods they no longer see everyone as "the enemy."

Will this reduce violent crime? So far, it's unclear. A 1981 study of police who switched from cars to foot patrol in Newark, New Jersey, showed no change in the crime rate. But the people felt safer. In a Houston, Texas, neighborhood, foot patrols did decrease crime, but crime in the next neighborhood went up.

We Saw It on TV

In 1991, a videotape of Los Angeles police beating a black man sickened the whole country. The man, Rodney King, was handcuffed. Police officers made him lie on the ground and then kicked and beat him with their clubs. A witness caught it with a camera and television news programs across the country showed the tape.

An independent investigation of the Los Angeles Police Department was launched in response to the incident. It found that "racism" and the use of "excessive force" were serious problems in the department.

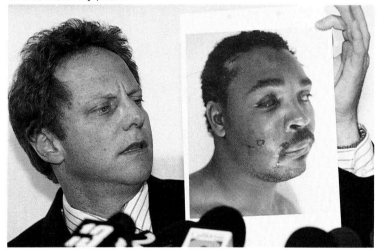

Steven Lerman, Rodney King's attorney, shows a photograph of King after he was beaten by police.

The Rodney King incident in Los Angeles sent a wave of horror across the nation. People were shocked by the officer's brutality in the videotape. Though harsh, the reality that was shown to viewers on the television screen spurred others to videotape incidents as proof of other injustices. In Fort Worth, Texas, a vacationing Ohio woman spotted a police officer subduing a suspect on Interstate 30. From 250 yards away, the woman videotaped as the officer viciously clubbed a handcuffed man more than twenty-four times on the head. The videotape was later used to suspend the officer.

How much of this happens when no one is around with a camera? Many police departments have set up programs to try to deal with problems like this. They aim to make the police more sensitive to what it's like to be poor or from a minority.

Police Brutality

The police are the foot soldiers in the fight against crime. They don't make the rules, but they are on the front line when violence occurs. Their job is tough and often requires them to risk their lives to do it. But sometimes they become part of the problem instead of the solution.

For example, a series of charges of brutality in the late 1980s were made against several police departments in Texas. In 1990, three white officers in the town of Hemphill were convicted of beating a black prisoner to death. They included the town's former chief of police.

Courts and the Police: Rights of the Accused

Freedom is something Americans have always held dear. The Constitution limits how much the government can interfere with our lives. These protections are in the Bill of Rights.

But in fighting crime, the police often need to take strong measures. They have to get evidence and bring the guilty to justice. Sometimes when they do this, they overdo it, violating our rights.

How far should the police be allowed to go in enforcing the law? When do their activities threaten our freedom? When does protecting the rights of the accused stop the police from doing their job—maybe even putting their own lives in danger? Where do we draw the line?

Until the 1960s, the police were not as carefully supervised as they are today. When investigating a crime, they themselves often disobeyed the law. In the 1960s, the

After the Rodney King beating, Los Angeles Police Chief Daryl Gates was sharply criticized for the brutality of his department.

The Supreme Court case against Ernesto Miranda in 1966 established a suspect's right "to remain silent" and other rights when taken into custody. These rights are today referred to as the Miranda rights.

Supreme Court made several important decisions on this subject. They said that the police needed to be more restrained.

For example, today the police need a search warrant before they can enter someone's house without their permission. The search warrant is a permit signed by a judge. The police have to convince the judge that they have good reason to suspect that there is evidence of a crime in the house. In the past, the police often got evidence without a proper warrant and judges allowed this evidence to be used in court to convict someone.

Before the 1960s, the police also used force to make people confess. In the station house, prisoners were hit and punched, made to go without sleep, and threatened with worse treatment. Only then could they call a lawyer. This was called the "third degree" and the courts looked the other way.

But in 1961, the Supreme Court ruled that no court could allow the use of evidence obtained illegally (*Mapp* v. *Ohio*). This held true even if what they found made it obvious that the suspect was guilty. Evidence obtained this way was to be excluded from the trial. (This was called the "exclusionary rule.")

In another case, in 1964, the court held that a suspect must not be questioned without being allowed to see a lawyer (*Escobedo* v. *Illinois*).

The most well known of these cases came in 1966: *Miranda* v. *Arizona*. Ernesto A. Miranda, who worked in a warehouse in Phoenix, had been arrested for rape and

Where's the "Bargain" in Plea Bargaining?

To many people, criminal courts seem to go about their business in a strange way. People are arrested and charged with serious crimes of violence only to be allowed to plead guilty to less serious offenses. The length of their sentence does not seem to match their crime. What's going on? Is this justice?

This practice is called plea bargaining. It's a deal in which the prisoner gets a softer sentence than he or she would if convicted on the original charge. In return, the state saves the expense of a trial.

Without plea bargaining, the criminal justice system would break down. There are not nearly enough judges or courtrooms to handle all the potential trials. Nor will there be money available to pay for them any time soon. If anything, cities and states have been cutting their budgets. So, imperfect as it is, plea bargaining is unavoidable.

What's more, there's no guarantee that a trial will bring a guilty verdict. Plea bargaining at least insures some punishment. And in very serious crimes, like murder,

plea bargaining is less likely to be used by the courts.

Because of public anger over plea bargaining, a different approach was tried. Where guns and drugs were involved, some states said that a guilty plea would bring a minimum prison term. But in response, more prisoners demanded trials. The courts couldn't handle the great increase in volume, so prosecutors made fewer arrests. That left more criminals on the streets. In the final analysis, nothing much changed.

kidnapping. He confessed, but was never told that he could choose not to make a statement; nor was he allowed to see a lawyer. In the *Miranda* case, the Court said that the police must inform a suspect of all his or her rights—such as the right to remain silent and to consult a lawyer—before questioning. Without this, any confession was worthless.

Reading suspects their "Miranda rights" became a common sight on television crime shows. Often a police officer would be shown handcuffing a prisoner as the officer read from a piece of paper: "You have the right to remain silent. You have the right to . . ."

By the late 1960s, many people felt that the Court had gone too far. To them, it seemed that the police were now the ones who were handcuffed. Many Americans felt that the courts were weakening the police just when crime was getting worse.

"Technicalities"

To many people, criminals seemed to be going free on "technicalities." They were getting off because the police had made minor mistakes. When the mistakes were discovered, the whole case was thrown out. Was the accused actually guilty? It didn't matter.

Defenders of the Supreme Court's decisions said that letting some people get off on minor points was worth it. It was the only way to preserve freedom for everyone. Curbing those freedoms could put us on the road to a police state. Society is not perfect. Some people will always take advantage of legal loopholes, but that's the risk we take in a democracy.

Others pointed out that the decisions didn't hurt police work anyway. For example, studies showed that criminals still confessed at about the same rate despite the *Miranda* decision.

In the original *Miranda* case, Miranda was retried and found guilty. The police didn't need his illegal confession.

Protecting his rights did not stop the wheels of justice.

But in response to public fears, presidents Nixon, Reagan, and Bush named more conservative justices to the Supreme Court. And they limited some decisions of the 1960s.

These judges have begun to look at some police mistakes as "harmless errors." Although such errors may make a particular piece of evidence unusable in court, they don't require that the whole case be thrown out. There can still be a guilty verdict if other evidence proves guilt. Such reasoning, for example, was the basis of the ruling in *Arizona* v. *Fulminante* in 1991, in which a conviction was allowed to stand even though a confession had been forced from the defendant.

Punishment

"People who commit violent crimes belong behind bars." Most people would probably agree with this. The problem is that there are not enough cells. New ones can cost as much as $75,000 each to build. Including food, medical care, and so on, it costs about as much to keep a person in a state prison each year as it does to send a student to an Ivy League college.

Should we just keep filling the cells? Isn't there a better way to make the prisons part of the fight against violent crime? A few ways have been suggested, but each has serious flaws.

One approach would be to focus on "career criminals." More than sixty percent of those released from state prisons are rearrested for serious crimes within three years. Shouldn't they get longer sentences? People not likely to break the law again could be given shorter sentences. Or maybe they could be put on probation. They would be supervised, but remain free. This would free cells for the most dangerous criminals.

But how do we predict who will commit more crimes? We don't have a reliable way of doing this. Even a long arrest record for a person doesn't prove anything. Some repeaters may simply get caught more often than others.

San Diego, California, made an attempt to zero in on career criminals. The conviction rate for repeat offenders increased. But the overall crime rate did not change.

What about people who commit crimes while out on bail? They are already awaiting trial for other crimes. In the 1980s, a Washington, D.C., law tried to deal with this. It provided for "preventive detention." At a hearing, a judge was to decide if someone arrested for a violent crime was a bad risk. If they were, no bail would be set. They would stay in jail until tried.

But these hearings got very involved, becoming like trials themselves. Besides, setting a high bail accomplished the same end. This kept many dangerous criminals locked up. However, it also violated the spirit of the law. Bail is supposed to guarantee that people show up for trials. It's not meant to keep them in jail.

Juvenile Justice

How about getting to criminals early in their career? Through the 1950s, the trend was to treat teenage criminals differently from adults. Offenders were sent to reformatories, and sentences were kept to a minimum.

By the 1980s, the juvenile justice system was changing. A series of court decisions gave young offenders some rights of adults. Youths accused of serious crimes also began to be punished as if they were adults. Some got regular prison terms.

However, this did not put a dent in the crime rate. And critics pointed out that what young criminals didn't know about crime already, they would certainly learn in prison.

A program in Massachusetts in the 1980s brought some good results. Young criminals, instead of being sent to jail, had to pay for damage they caused and help people they hurt. But public anger at juvenile crime in the rest of the country kept this idea from spreading.

The Death Penalty

Perhaps the most popular response in America to violent crime is to call for greater use of the death penalty. Those who support it say that it will stop criminals from killing. They will think twice if they know that they could die for their crime. Supporters also say that anyone who takes a life ought to lose theirs in return. Public support for the death penalty rose from about fifty percent in the early 1970s to about eighty percent today.

Opponents say that it is brutal to punish someone this way, no matter what they have done. It brings society down to the level of the criminal. It's the only punishment that can't be reversed if the person is later proved innocent. And it is most often those who are poor and black who receive a death sentence.

In 1972 the Supreme Court temporarily halted the use of capital punishment because it was not being applied in a fair way. It was not handed out for the same crimes by each judge. A death sentence depended too much on

The Florida execution in 1989 of convicted mass murderer Ted Bundy brought discussion of the death penalty to the forefront of the news.

which judge was on the bench. It could even be affected by what kind of mood he or she was in that day.

The states responded with new laws that spelled out when the death penalty was to be used. Executions resumed in 1977.

Since then, debate has raged over the appeal process as well as the punishment itself. Prisoners spent years on death row while their lawyers filed one appeal after another. Often these appeals seemed based on minor legal details. Many people felt that this defeated the purpose of the death penalty. It was being handed down, but not carried out.

But the appeals involved more than that. Many had to do with the poverty and race of the prisoners. A good courtroom lawyer can cost about $1,000 a day. Of the 2,400 people on death row in 1991, about ninety percent could not afford a lawyer at their trial. And lawyers appointed by the court may not be as good as the kind you can hire yourself.

Another major theme in the appeals is race. The statistics appear to show that American society values the life of a white person more than it does that of a black. When Donald (Peewee) Gaskins was executed in South Carolina in 1991 for killing a black man, it was the first time a white had been executed anywhere in the United States for murdering a black since 1944.

Still, the public does not want appeals to drag on, and the Supreme Court has recently limited them. In 1987 the Court made it harder for lawyers to appeal on the grounds of racial bias. In 1989 it ruled that states did not have to pay for a prisoner's appeals. States only had to provide a lawyer for the original trial. And in 1991, the Court curbed appeals on technicalities.

And what is the effect of capital punishment on violent crime? Does the death penalty deter it? No conclusive proof exists either way. We simply do not know for sure. The debate continues.

Opposite:
Death by electrocution is one of the most commonly used methods of capital punishment.

New Solutions to Old Problems

A number of troubling problems have worsened significantly in America over the past ten years. Teenage crime, overcrowding of prisons, and police brutality are just a few of America's most pressing concerns. In response to these troubles, many cities and states across the country are experimenting with a number of new programs that are designed to ease these problems.

Curfews

Every so often a city sets a curfew for teenagers. This usually follows an outbreak of crimes committed by young people who seemed to be "out of control." Curfews are supposed to take teenagers off the streets before they are tempted to get into trouble. For example, in 1990, Atlanta, Georgia, decreed that teenagers under the age of seventeen had to be home by eleven on weeknights and by midnight on weekends. Furthermore, parents of teenagers who violate this law can be held responsible for their child's behavior and receive a fine or jail term.

The American Civil Liberties Union charged that this curfew was aimed at poor, black neighborhoods. They also said that the law violates the rights of young people. One teenager complained: "What's the difference between a sixteen-year-old and a seventeen-year-old, and why should there be a curfew for one and not the other?"

Do curfews work? Many police departments say they do. But there is no evidence for their long-term success. In fact, Atlanta had a curfew program in the early 1980s but let it lapse.

Neighborhood Block-Watch Groups

Another way residential communities are striving to combat crime in their areas is through the creation of "block-watch" associations. Working together, residents of a neighborhood participate in a program where everyone watches out for everyone else. Heightened awareness of home safety and crime prevention techniques is usually accompanied by regular meetings that update residents on recent developments in the neighborhood. In addition, each block-watch group establishes a direct line of communication with their police department. This makes reporting crime more efficent and response by police more effective.

New Techniques for Police Officers

Police departments have recently begun a number of programs to make their organizations more effective. Among these new strategies are adaptable city patrols that

Neighborhood watch groups have become a popular way for communities to band together for safety and crime prevention.

include downtown surveillance on bicycles, returning to the "neighborhood beat" approach where officers get to know the residents and problems of a specific community, and establishing closer ties to schools and other youth centers in order to keep better informed of potential problems.

Many police departments are also experimenting with video cameras in squad cars as a means by which to record arrests and on-site interrogations. Running a video camera during arrests would work to protect both the police and those they apprehend. With the camera running, officers are much less likely to use excessive force or other abusive tactics. At the same time, a videotaped record of an arrest can prove that proper procedures were followed and can help to avoid false charges of misconduct.

The New Prisoner

To combat the unprecedented rise in prison and jail overcrowding, some states are using technology that allows prisoners to be outside the walls of a prison while remaining in custody. The most common form of this "criminal tracking system" works like an electric homing device. Prisoners are outfitted with a small "box" that transmits a signal to a central prison location. There, the whereabouts and activities of a prisoner can be monitored. This system, though practical only for a limited number of the country's least dangerous criminals, has helped to ease overcrowding in some of America's most populated facilities.

Video cameras placed in squad cars will record the details of arrests and questioning.

An electric home detention device is attached to the leg of a prisoner. The device transmits a signal to a central office where activities are monitored by computer.

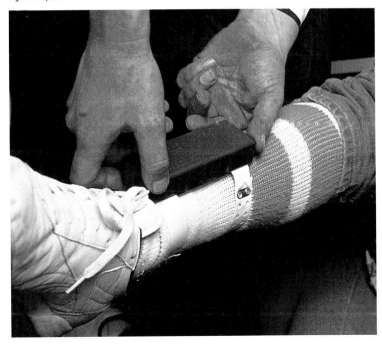

Chapter 5

Solutions from Washington

Although most crime-fighting occurs on the state and city level, the national government is not above the battle. In fact, the sounds of anti-crime combat come like a steady drum beat from Washington—especially on the issue of drugs.

About twenty-eight million Americans use illegal drugs each year. Presidents Nixon, Reagan and Bush have declared "war" on drugs. We have an anti-drug "czar," a federal official to lead the fight. Slogans on everything from milk cartons to billboards enlist everyone in the struggle. We even invaded Panama and arrested its leader, Manuel Noriega, charging him with trading in drugs like a common criminal.

Yet with all the fire and smoke, where are the victories? And how can this war be won when even the generals sometimes go over to the other side? Mayor Marion Barry of Washington, D.C., was a leader of the anti-drug effort. That ended with his arrest and conviction for possession of crack in 1990.

Federal Anti-Drug Activity

Narcotics are involved in one way or another in many violent crimes. Most of the drug supply comes in from

Lawmakers continue to battle over proposed gun-control legislation and other anti-crime measures

Opposite:
James Brady, in the wheelchair, has been one of Washington's most vigorous proponents of gun control.

In 1989, U.S. troops invaded Panama and captured its leader, Manuel Noriega. President Bush said the invasion was meant to disrupt a major drug trading network centered in Panama.

abroad and crosses state lines. This gives the federal government, not just the states, the power to act.

Richard Nixon was the first president to declare a war on drugs. His idea was to cut crime by decreasing drug use in the United States. Stopping the supply smuggled in from abroad was the main aim of this program. Funds also went toward educating young people not to use drugs.

The Power of the Cali Cartel

José Santacruz Londono used to be a small-time criminal in Colombia. Now he is known as Don Chepe, a billionaire whose marble mansion sits high above the sugarcane fields of Cali, Colombia's third-largest city. A few miles away, in the rich suburb of Ciudad Jardin, is the luxurious compound of Gilberto Rodriguez Orejuela, known as the "Chess Player." He, too, is one of Colombia's richest men. Together, the Londonos and the Orejuelas are among the richest and most powerful families in all of South America. Where does this amazing wealth come from?

These two families represent the center of the world cocaine market. Bigger, better organized, and better protected than the Sicilian Mafia, the "Cali cartel" seems almost unstoppable. (A cartel is a powerful group that controls a particular market or product.) Robert Bonner, administrator of the U.S. Drug Enforcement Adminsitration (DEA) says, "The Cali cartel is the most powerful criminal organization in the world. No drug organization rivals them today or perhaps anytime in history."

According to the DEA, the Cali cartel today produces seventy percent of the cocaine that reaches the United States. They produce ninety percent of the cocaine that fuels the European market. The two Cali godfathers have a virtual lock on the world wholesale market of the drug, perhaps the most profitable product ever to be handled by members of organized crime.

In the 1980s, most of the world cocaine trade was controlled by a cartel in another Colombian city, Medellín. But the power of Medellín has been shattered in recent years by its fierce battles with the Colombian government. Counterattacks from Colombian authorities succeeded in killing drug boss José Gonzalo Rodriguez Gacha and forced the surrender of many of his top people. The most stunning blow to the Medellín power base was the surrender in 1991 of Medellín drug chief Pablo Escobar Gaviria to Colombian authorities. They promised Gaviria he would not stand trial in the United States.

Just when Colombian authorities managed to disrupt and damage what was the world's most powerful drug cartel, another cartel, in Cali, was poised to take its place. The Cali organization has insulated itself from government interference through political influence, bribery, and threat of violence.

Today, drug enforcement officials say that Cali is responsible for the importation of four out of every five grams of cocaine sold on the streets of New York City. The percentage is even higher for some European cities. The Cali families are now focusing their efforts on expanding their global markets. They have recently targeted the high-income consumers in Japan and the Netherlands.

Pablo Escobar Gaviria, ex-chief of the Medellín drug cartel.

Though U.S. officials have made some progress battling the Cali cartel, their victories have not stopped the steady growth of its empire. Drug enforcement officials from around the world are now turning their attention to battling the Cali organization more strongly. But each day that passes brings only greater strength and continued success for what is now the world's most powerful and despicable drug empire.

Spurred by the arrival of crack in the mid-1980s, President Reagan increased the pace of the campaign. Attention focused on Latin America as the source of cocaine. The plant from which it comes is grown mostly in Bolivia and Peru. Cocaine is refined in and shipped from Panama and Colombia.

In 1989, the United States invaded Panama. One reason given was to stop the drug trade. Manuel Noriega, who controlled the government, was brought to the United States to be tried, but the drug trade went on.

The United States wanted Colombia to curb its big drug gangs, called cartels. The Colombian government said that the big demand for drugs in the United States was the real problem. But Colombia did agree to clamp down on the cartels, and it sent some drug traders to the United States to be tried.

The Wrong Emphasis?

In the United States, spending for the war on drugs has reached $11 billion a year. But only about five percent of that goes toward treating addicts. Many critics say that this is the wrong emphasis. They claim that we need to go to the root of the problem: the user. This would be cheaper as well as better. It costs about $25,000 a year to keep an addict in prison, but at most about $15,000 per year to treat him or her.

Others want to legalize drugs. They say this would break the connection between the drug trade and crime. They point out that Prohibition was similar to today's drug trade. Making alcohol illegal created violence that wasn't there before. Repealing Prohibition ended the violence. But so far legalizing drugs has little public support.

The war on drugs continues, but victory does not appear in sight. Tougher laws against selling drugs have even created new problems. In 1990, a congressional study warned that drug cases were seriously overwhelming the courts.

Gun Control

What about federal laws to reduce access to guns? "Cop-killing" bullets that can pierce bullet-proof vests are illegal. Machine guns have also been banned. But lobbyists representing the millions who don't want the law to go any further than that had their way through the beginning of the 1990s.

The issue of gun control continues to divide the Congress and the country each year. The National Rifle Association, which opposes gun control, represents the views of millions of Americans and is one of the strongest lobbies in Washington.

VIOLENT CRIMES AT A GLANCE

Percentage of murders committed with handguns

1980: 43.4%

1989: 41.9%

• Percentage of those arrested for murder who go to prison: **53**

1990 increase in reports of violent crimes by region

South: 13%

Midwest: 12%

Northeast: 6%

West: 9%

• Violent-crime victims who receive help from authorities: **11%**

Public's view of best way to reduce crime:

More executions

33%

More crime-prevention measures

65%

Source: U.S. News and World Report, May 6, 1991.

"Guns don't kill people. People kill people," say those opposed to gun control. Should cars be banned because accidents kill 50,000 a year in the United States?

"People *try* to kill people. Guns kill people best," argue those who support gun control. That's especially true when it comes to handguns. If we had a federal law regulating guns, people couldn't simply go to another place to get one when their own city passed a law against them.

Because buying a gun is easier in some cities—such as Miami and Los Angeles—they have become centers for weapon sales. In fact, this has undermined the war on

Washington and Gun Control

When shots were fired at Ronald Reagan in 1981, James Brady was standing near the president. It was then that Brady, the president's press secretary, was shot in the head. Remarkably, Brady survived, though he was permanently disabled. Since that day, James Brady and his wife have lobbied strenuously to make gun control a top priority for all of Washington's lawmakers.

The Brady Bill

In 1991—ten years after the assassination attempt—James Brady finally got some satisfaction. A gun control law, commonly known as the Brady Bill, was approved by both the House and the Senate. Word then came from the White House that President Bush would sign an anticrime package that included the Brady Bill measures.

The law proposed a five- to seven-day waiting period for the purchase of firearms. This waiting period would give gun shops time to check into the backgrounds of potential buyers and would reduce the chances of someone buying a gun "in the heat of passion or rage."

Action in Congress on gun control is the result of many conflicting elements. On one hand, both Democrats and Republicans are eager to convince voters that they are "tough on crime." At the same time, those same politicians are faced with the fierce and extremely influential lobbying efforts of anti-gun-control factions; most notably, the National Rifle Association (NRA). In addition, the issue of gun control deeply divides Americans across the nation. "There are enormous regional differences on the issue," said Celinda Lake, a poll taker who has conducted a number of crime-issue surveys for both Democrats and Republicans. "Getting the upper hand on this issue is different on the coasts, in the West, and in the middle of this country."

The Tragedy in Killeen

Many lawmakers attempted to go the Brady Bill one better in October 1991. It was then that a nationwide ban was proposed on semiautomatic weapons. The ban proposed that thirteen models of assault-style weapons be outlawed. Then a tragic but incredible coincidence occurred. The day before the vote was to be taken on the ban, the worst mass shooting in American history took place.

On October 16, 1991, George Hennard drove his blue pickup truck through the window of a crowded cafeteria in Killeen, Texas. He then got out of his truck and opened fire on the crowd with two semiautomatic pistols before killing himself. When it was all over, twenty-three people lay dead and many others were injured.

On October 17, lawmakers assembled on Capitol Hill to vote on the proposed semiautomatic weapons ban. Despite the tragedy of the day before, lawmakers voted 247–177 to strike down the measure. Ironically, if the proposal had been in place on October 16, there would have been a ban on ammunition clips containing more than seven bullets each. With a maximum of seven bullets in a clip, George Hennard would have had to stop to reload a number of times; that might have saved lives.

When asked about limiting gun sales in light of the Killeen mass shooting, President Bush said, "Obviously, when you see somebody go berserk and get a weapon and go in and murder people, of course, it troubles me. But what I don't happen to have the answer to is, can you legislate that behavior away."

Mayhem ensues just seconds after shots were fired at President Ronald Reagan and James Brady in 1981.

drugs. The Colombian drug cartels buy guns in Miami. In 1989, they used them to kill three presidential candidates in their own country.

Efforts to tighten control on the sale of guns have met strong resistance. The three-million-member National Rifle Association has led the fight. Among its members are many prominent Americans, including George Bush.

But as the 1990s began, support was building for some kind of law to stop the shooting. In fact, more than seventy percent of Americans favor tighter gun control laws. And it's likely that we will have stricter laws soon.

Conclusion

The problem of violent crime wasn't always this bad. It developed in response to changes in American society. Since society is always changing, won't crime change with it? Isn't it possible that violent crime might just decline by itself over time?

This may yet happen, especially if the crack epidemic fades. In the meantime, we might be able to help move it in the right direction.

The get-tough approach to violent crime that began in the 1970s hasn't worked. Changing the way we use the police, sending more people to prison, and getting tougher in court have not done the job.

Anti-poverty measures tried in the 1960s didn't do it either. But there may be better ways of reducing poverty, strengthening families, providing jobs for people—and better ways to deal with drugs. These would involve prevention more than trying to deal with violence after it happens.

A well-known conservative who often writes about crime has said as much. James Q. Wilson wrote: "If you wish to make a big difference in crime rates, you must make a fundamental change in society."

What kind of change? That's a big question. It's one we have yet to answer.

Chronology

1920s Prohibition of alcohol spawns a crime wave.

Chicago's Al Capone is kingpin of the illegal liquor trade.

1930s Bank robbers like John Dillinger and Bonnie and Clyde cause another crime wave.

1940s World War II; increase in teenage crime is reported.

1940s and 1950s Gangs, including the Mafia, fight over control of the sale of narcotics.

1946–1964 The "baby boom" years. A large number of births occurred.

1950s Problems of juvenile delinquency grow.

1960–1981 Reported serious crimes increase more than two-hundred percent.

1961 The Supreme Court rules that no court can use evidence obtained illegally.

1964 Republican presidential candidate Barry Goldwater makes violent crime a major political issue.

The Supreme Court rules that no suspect may be questioned without being allowed to see a lawyer.

Mid-1960s Riots break out in many inner cities.

Civil rights movement brings more freedoms for blacks.

President Lyndon Johnson says American cities are becoming "places of terror." Laws are passed making many kinds of discrimination illegal.

1966 The Supreme Court case against Ernesto Miranda establishes suspect's rights.

1968 Republican presidential candidate Richard Nixon says he wants to "end crime in the streets."

1969–1990 The number of children growing up in poverty increases fifty percent.

Early 1970s First reports of coca-paste use come from Peru.

1971 Philadelphia police commissioner Frank Rizzo is elected mayor.

1972 The Supreme Court temporarily halts capital punishment. Executions resume in 1977.

1973 President Nixon calls drugs "public enemy number one."

1979 Curtis Sliwa founds the Guardian Angels in New York City.

1980s Federal prison population doubles.

Drug cartel in Medellín, Colombia, controls most of the world's cocaine trade.

1980 Crack first hits Los Angeles.

1983 "Rock houses" appear in certain L.A. neighborhoods.

1984 Use of crack in American cities skyrockets to incredible proportions.

1984–1988 Murder rate for black youths ages fifteen to nineteen doubles.

1985–1989 Murder rate in Washington, D.C., increases 151% after introduction of crack.

The National Cocaine Hotline estimates that over one million Americans have tried crack.

1987–1991	The Supreme Court puts limitations on appeals.
1989	The United States invades Panama and captures leader Manuel Noriega.
1990s	Violent crime increases eleven percent.
	One out of every one thousand black males fifteen to twenty-four is being murdered.
	23,438 murders, 102,555 rapes, and 639,271 robberies are reported in the United States.
	Federal prisons hold 65,526 inmates. Federal penitentiaries hold 705,717.
	Congressional study warns that drug cases are overwhelming the courts.
1991	Crips and Bloods are known to be in thirty-two states and 113 cities.
	The Supreme Court allows a conviction to stand even though a confession was forced from the defendant.
	Medellín drug chief Pablo Escobar Gaviria surrenders to Colombian authorities; Cali cartel takes over.

For Further Reading

Barden R. *Gangs.* Vero Beach: Rourke, 1991.

Barden, R. *Gun Control.* Vero Beach: Rourke, 1991.

Berger, Gilda. *Violence and Drugs.* New York: Franklin Watts, 1989.

Flanders, Carl N. *Capital Punishment.* New York: Facts On File, 1991.

Hays, S. *Capital Punishment.* Vero Beach: Rourke, 1991.

Landau, Elaine. *Teenage Violence.* Englewood Cliffs, NJ: Julian Messner, 1990.

Landes, Alison, Mark A. Siegel, and Carol D. Foster, eds. *Crime: A Serious American Problem.* Wylie, Texas: Information Plus, 1990.

LeVert, Marianne. *Crime in America.* New York: Facts On File, 1991.

Nash, Jay Robert. *Encyclopedia of World Crime.* North Bellmore: Marshall Cavendish, 1990.

Wright, Kevin. *The Great American Crime Myth.* Westport, CT: Greenwood Press, 1985.

Index